Easy Pea
All-in-One Homeschool

EP
Preschool
Printables

Color Edition

All-in-One
Homeschool

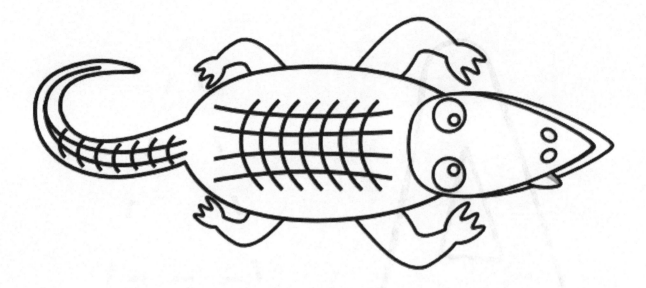

A a a

April
the
Alligator

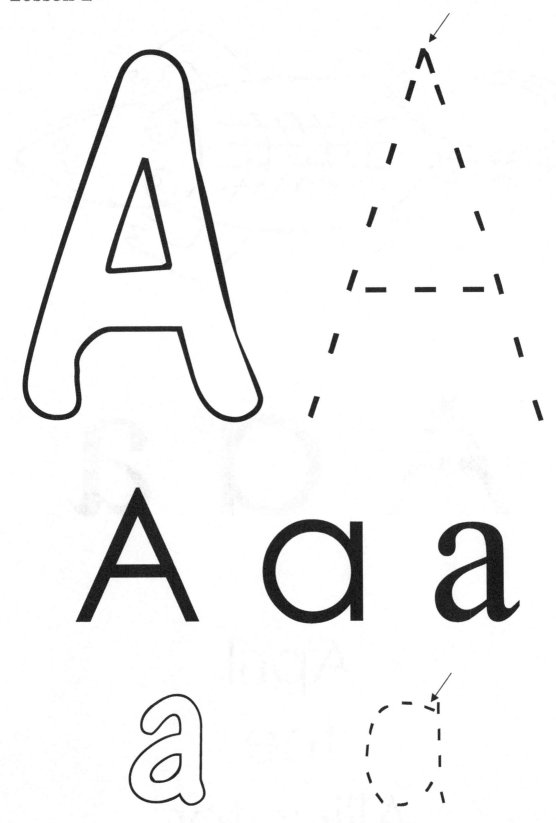

Cut out the alligator pieces in chunks and glue them onto a separate piece of paper. You can hold the paper up over your face and be the alligator's voice saying, "Aaaa!"

This page is blank for the cutting activity on the other side.

Cut out the two apple pieces.
Glue the core on the back of the
other. If you want, glue a piece
of string in between them.
Spin or flip it to see the
apple change.

This page is blank for the cutting activity on the other side.

Bb

Betty
the
Bee

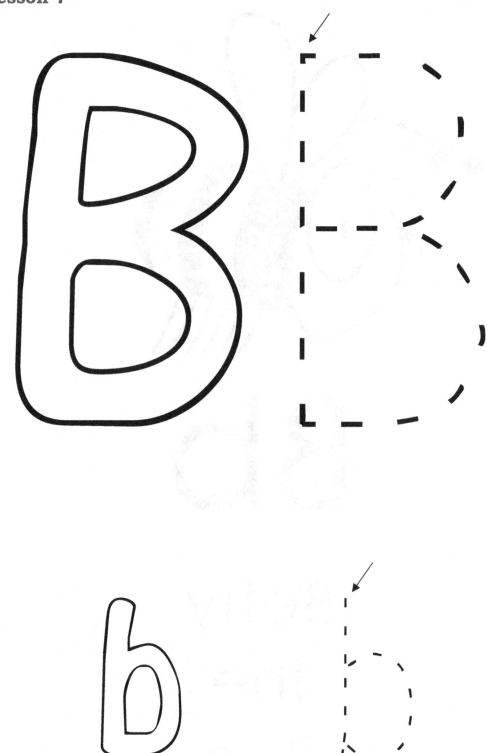

B b

Find the letters.

Black Bears live in forests and can climb trees. Black bears aren't always black. They can be brown, too. They like to eat berries and fish.

This page is blank for the cutting activity on the next page.

Cut out this bee. Trace your hands on a separate piece of paper and cut them out. Attach them to this bee as its wings. You can pretend it's a tired bee saying, "Buh, buh, buh." You could use it to act out the story.

This page is blank for the cutting activity on the other side.

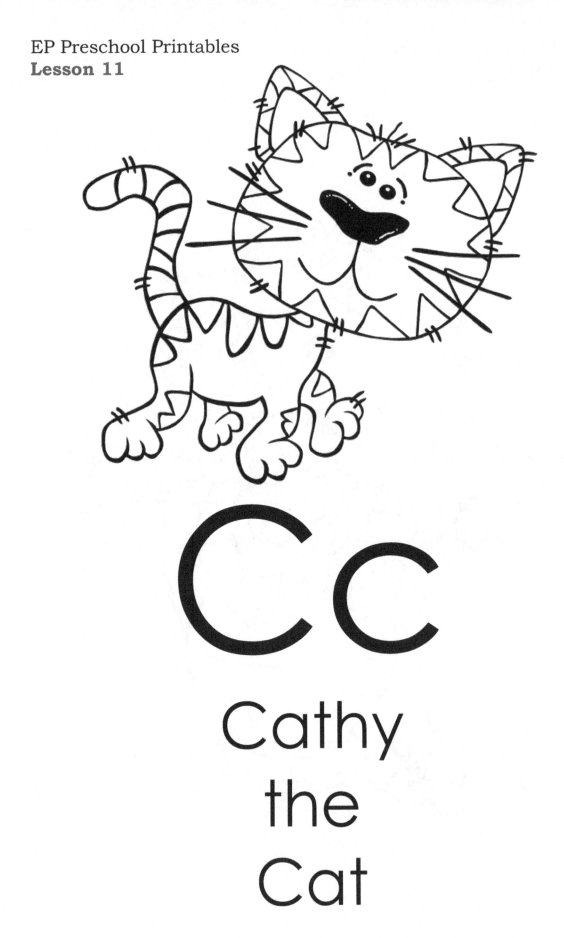

Cc

Cathy
the
Cat

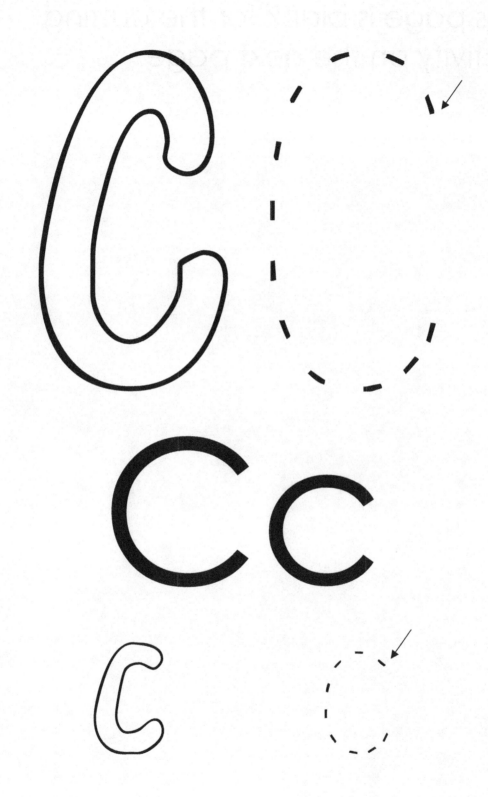

This page is blank for the cutting activity on the next page.

Cut out this cat. Cut out each box. Glue one cat onto the back of the other. Cut each of the two double-sided cats down the middle: one top down to the top of its nose and one from the bottom up to the top of its nose. Line up the slits with the papers perpendicular and slide them together to make a 3D cat. There's a second page of these.

This page is blank for the cutting activity on the other side.

Lesson 13

Cut out this cat. Cut out each box. Glue one cat onto the back of the other. Cut each of the two double-sided cats down the middle: one top down to the top of its nose and one from the bottom up to the top of its nose. Line up the slits with the papers perpendicular and slide them together to make a 3D cat.

This page is blank for the cutting activity on the other side.

Here's another "C" word to color. What is the "C" word?

Use blue to color in the circle however you like.

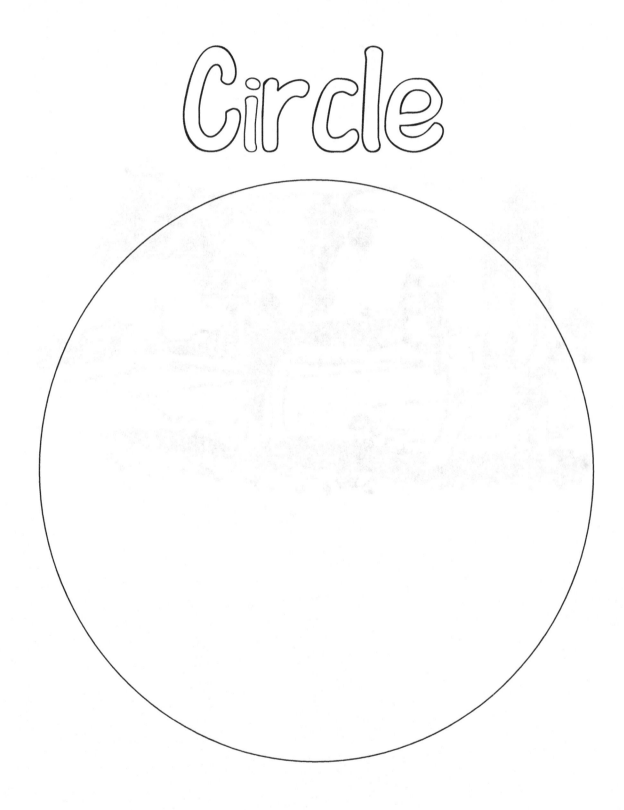

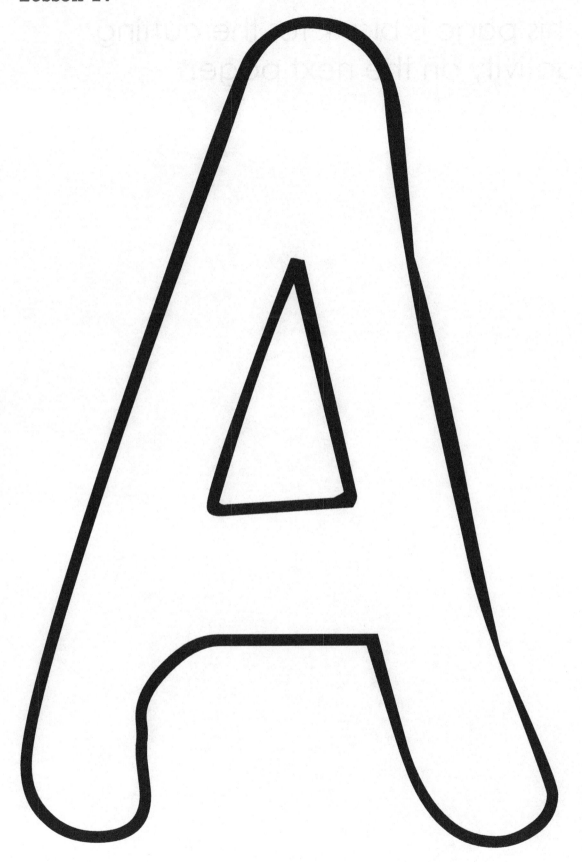

This page is blank for the cutting activity on the next page.

My
Circle
Book

Cut out the circles. Staple them together. Draw circles on your circles. You are making a circle book!

This page is blank for the cutting activity on the other side.

A a

Find the letters.

Many animals, such as the apes
in the picture above, live in the
wild. All animals have special
habitats where they like to live.

EP Preschool Printables
Lesson 18

This page is blank for the cutting activity on the next page.

Cut out the circles. Glue the circles to the head to add ears, eyes, and nose. Here's an example.

31

This page is blank for the cutting activity on the other side.

Trace the letter with your finger and then color it in blue. What does it say?

Sing the alphabet song. Practice the "C" sound. Find and mark each place you see an uppercase and lowercase letter C.

C c

Caribou are also known as reindeer. They are found in the Arctic where it is very cold. Can you see what's on its head?

Use blue to trace the circles.

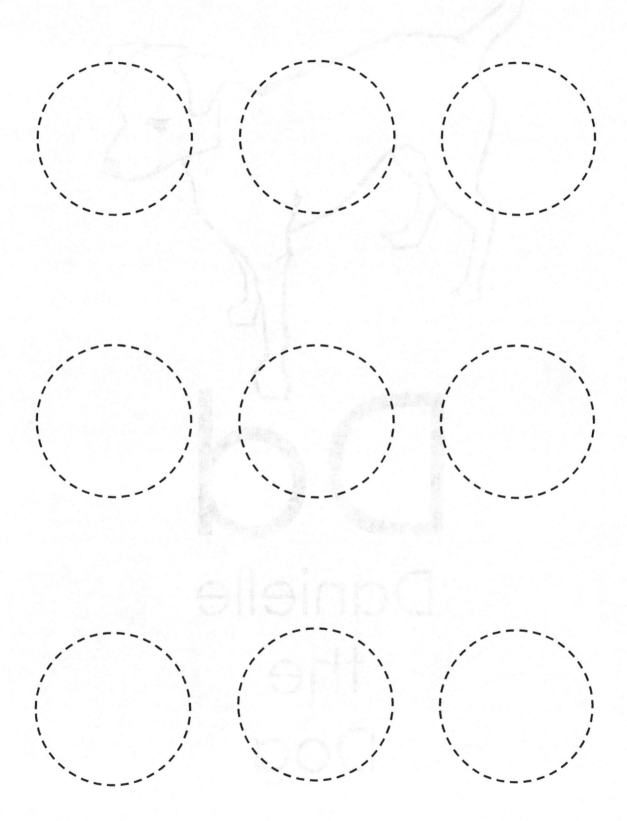

Dd

Danielle
the
Dog

Find every letter D, uppercase or lowercase, and color them in. There are three to find.

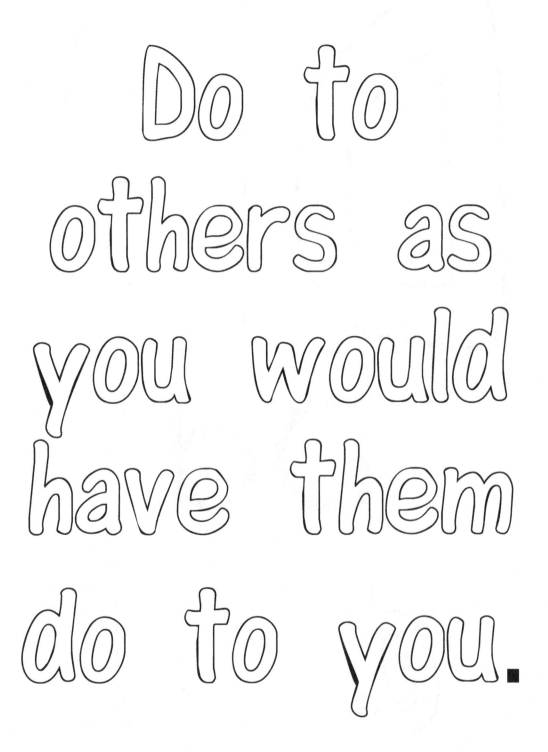

Do to others as you would have them do to you.

D d

Find the letters.

Dolphins live in the ocean. They have curved mouths that make them look friendly. They can be trained to do tricks.

40

Cut out these circles and glue them together into a dog picture. What does the dog and the letter D say?

41

This page is blank for the cutting activity on the other side.

Ee

Elizabeth
the
Elephant

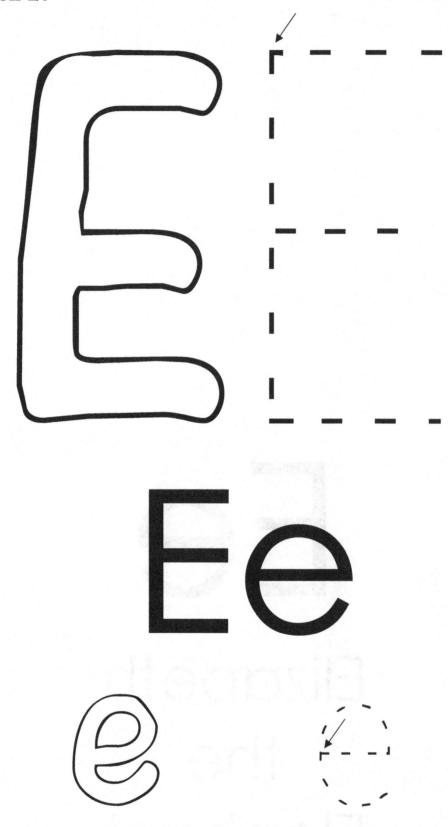

Find every letter E, uppercase or lowercase, and color them in. There are seven to find.

Every good gift and every perfect gift is from above.

Trace each line. Start at the smiley face and draw down. Then pick up your pencil or crayon and jump up to the next smiley face.

Here are some eggs to cut out. First, decorate them. Then cut them out and hide them for each other to find. Why are we cutting out eggs? What sound do they start with? What letter does the word "egg" start with?

This page is blank for the cutting activity on the other side.

Find the blank circle and color it in blue. Then cut out all of the circles and glue them onto a page to make a blue circle masterpiece! Maybe you'd like to draw more blue circles onto your artwork after you put these on.

This page is blank for the cutting activity on the other side.

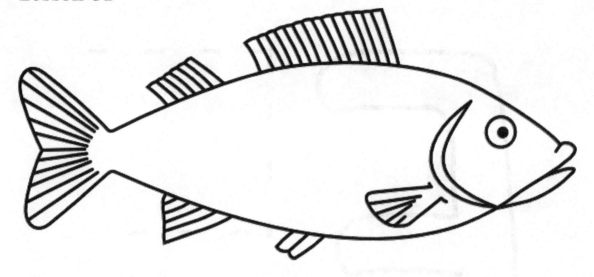

F f

Faith
the
Fish

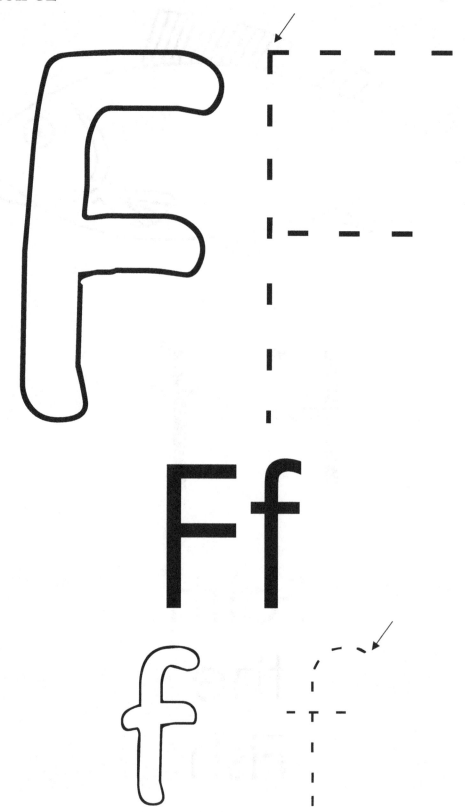

F f

Find the letters.

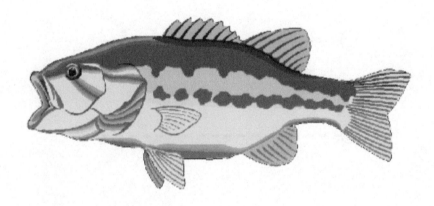

Fish come in many shapes and sizes. They swim free in oceans, seas, lakes, and rivers. Have you ever gone fishing? Do you eat fried fish?

Trace each line. Start at the smiley face and draw across. Then pick up your pencil or crayon and jump up to the next smiley face.

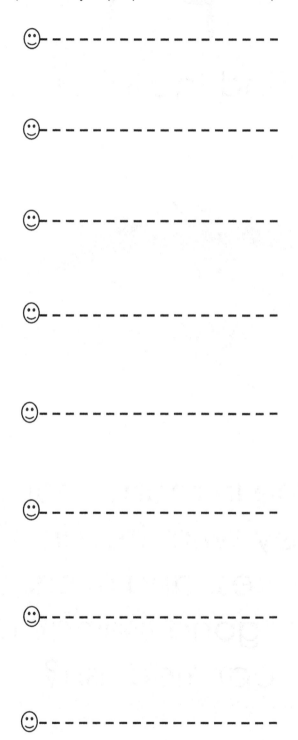

Find and color in every letter F that you find. There are three to find. Listen again to the story of Faith the Fish from Lesson 31. What does "F" say?

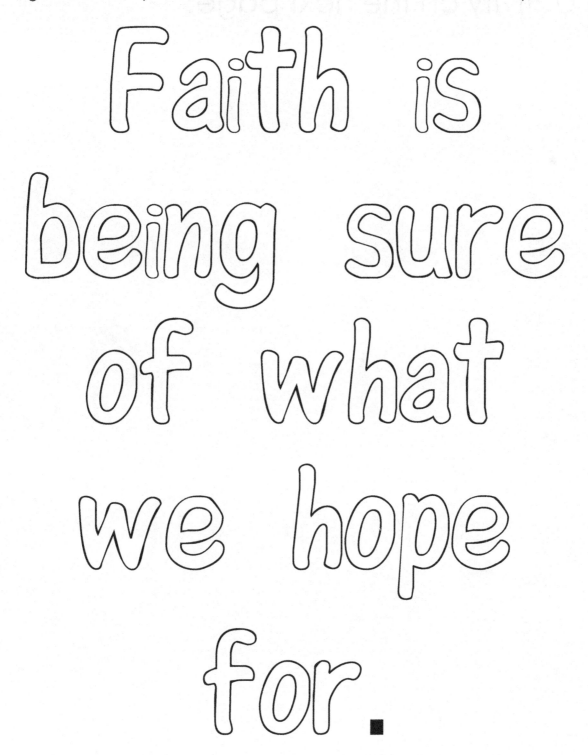

This page is blank for the cutting activity on the next page.

Make a Christmas tree. Cut out the triangles. Glue them together to make a tree and then decorate it. You can use the circles if you like.

This page is blank for the cutting activity on the next page.

E e
Find the letters.

African elephants are the largest land animals on Earth. They have bigger ears than Asian elephants.

This page is blank for the cutting activity on the next page.

Make a triangle fish. You can decorate your fish. What letter does fish start with? What sound?

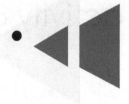

This page is blank for the cutting activity on the other side.

G g g

Greg
the
Goat

Give thanks with a grateful heart for God is good and righteous.

Trace each line. Start at the smiley face and draw down. Then pick up your pencil or crayon and jump up to the next smiley face.

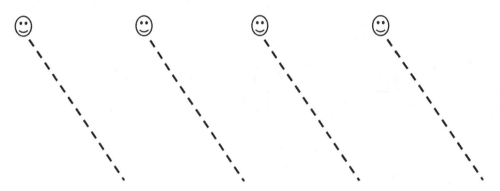

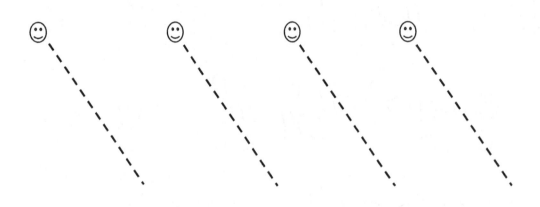

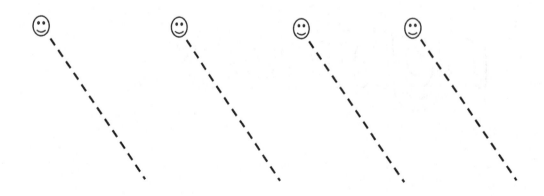

G g
Find the letters.

Gazelles live in the grasslands. They live in groups and can move very fast. Gazelles have hooves on their feet.

Make a bunch of grapes. Feel free to draw on grapes instead of doing all the cutting.

This page is blank for the cutting activity on the other side.

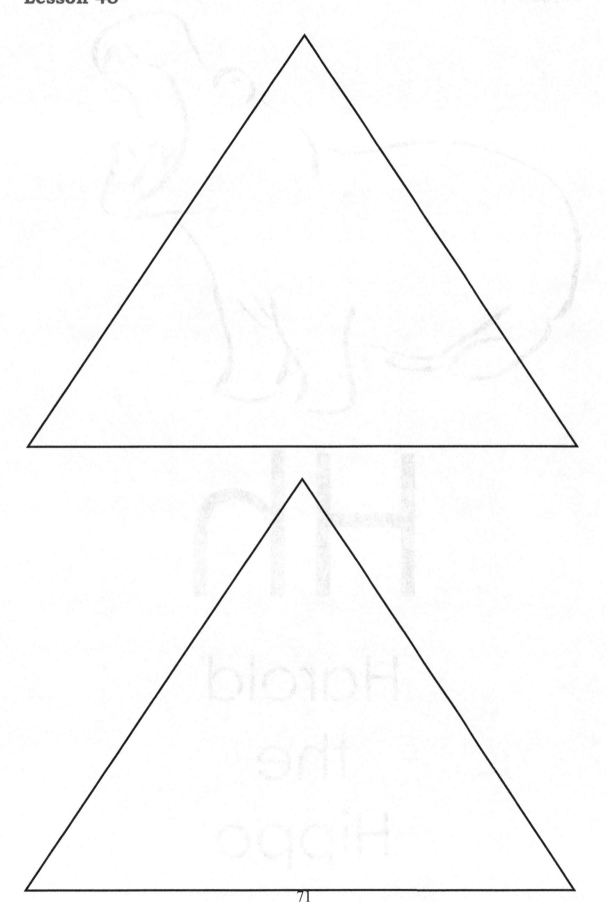

Hh

Harold
the
Hippo

How beautiful are the feet of those who bring the good news that the God of Israel reigns!

Take a pencil or a crayon and start at the first smiley face in the top left. Draw down. Then pick up your hand and jump back up to the next smiley face next to it.

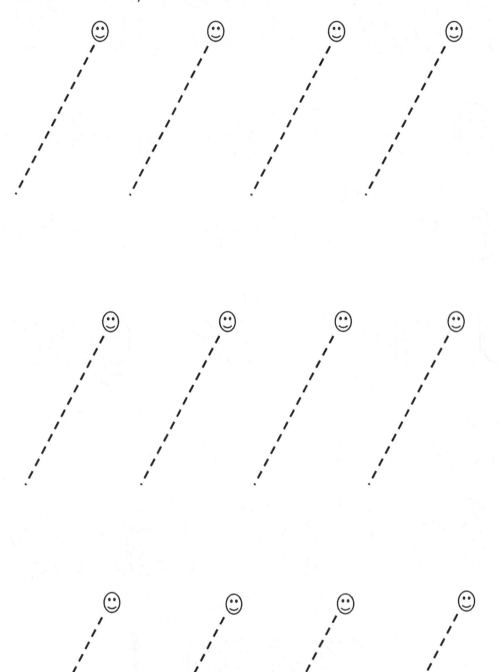

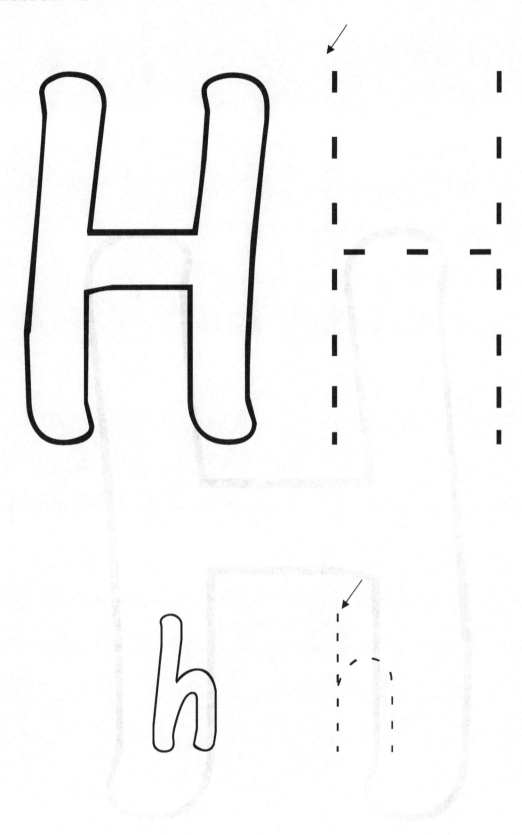

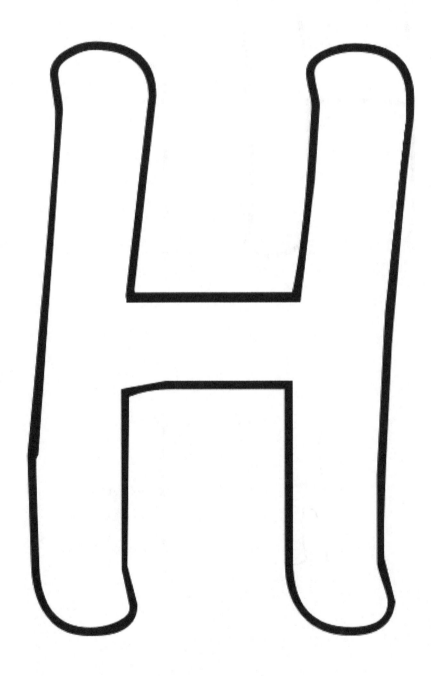

Trace your hand on this page. Hand starts with H. If you like, trace it with the fingers pointing down so that you can turn it into a horse. The fingers are the four legs and the thumb is the head.

Ii
Isaac
the
Iguana

Find the seven places where there is a Letter I and color them in.

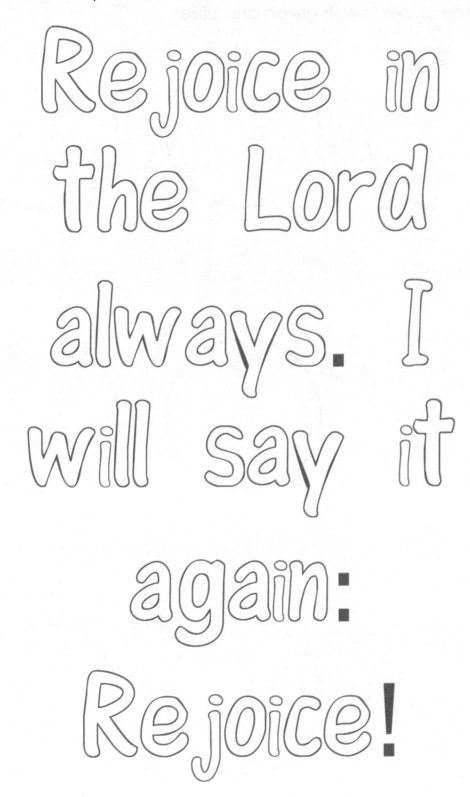

EP Preschool Printables
Lesson 52
Trace the circles starting at the smiley face in the top left and draw around the circle. Then move to the next circle. You can color the circles in with green and blue.

EP Preschool Printables
Lesson 53

Read the letters below. Then trace the dotted lines starting at the arrow. Make sure to go down first and then pick up your hand and jump to the top. For the capital letter, you will need one more jump to get to the bottom.

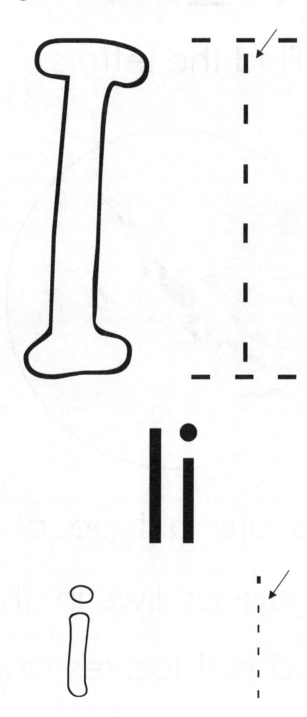

I i

Find the letters.

Iguanas are a type of lizard.

Green iguanas live in the rain

forest and eat leaves and fruit.

They are excellent swimmers.

Connect the dots in the order of the alphabet.

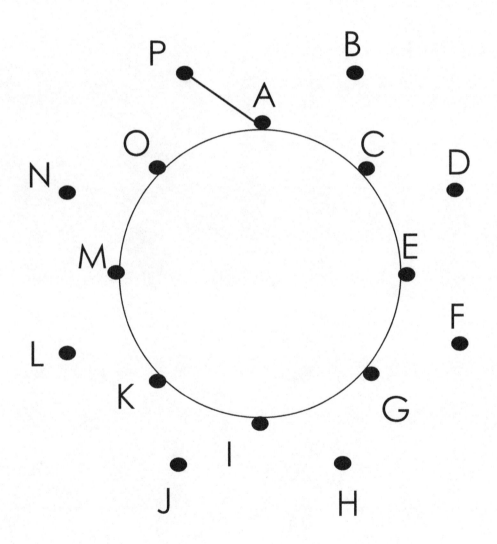

This page is blank for the cutting activity on the next page.

Draw triangles on these triangles or just color them green and blue and cut them out. Staple them together to make a triangle book.

This page is blank for the cutting activity on the other page.

H h

Find the letters.

Horses live in North America as well as in other continents. The hair on the back of their head is called a mane.

Find and color the squares.

Color the square red.

This page is blank for the cutting activity on the other side.

Color the circles red, the squares blue, and the triangles green. Someone older can cut out the circle and then you can cut out the shapes and glue them on to make a wreath.

This page is blank for the cutting activity on the other side.

Jj

John
the
Jaguar

The birth of Jesus Christ took place in just this way. His mother Mary had been engaged to Joseph.

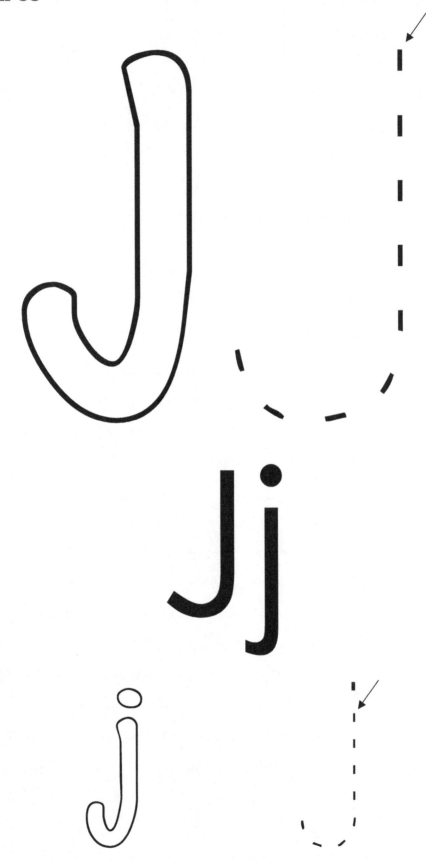

J j

Find the letters.

Jellyfish live in the ocean. They

journey along ocean currents.

Some jellyfish use jets to move

themselves in the water.

This page is blank for the cutting activity on the next page.

Can you act out "J" words? Jiggle, jump, jolt, jumble, jerk. Color in these shapes, blue, red, and green. Build them together into a Jack-in-the-Box. The square is the box. The rectangle is the lid. The triangle is the body, and the circle is the head. Feel free to decorate!

This page is blank for the cutting activity on the other side.

Kk

Keith
the
Kangaroo

O give thanks
to the LORD,
for He is good;
For His
lovingkindness
is everlasting.

Trace each line starting at the top left. Put your pencil or crayon on the smiley face. Trace the line. Then pick up your hand and move it to the next smiley face next to it.

This page is blank for the cutting activity on the next page.

Here is a kaleidoscope. Cut around it as a circle. Then cut it in half each way to make four pieces. Connect them all at the center point with a brass fastener or with a paper clip by opening the paper clip on one end and poking it through and then folding it down. Spin the pieces of the kaleidoscope.

This page is blank for the cutting activity on the other side.

Listen again to the story of Keith the Kangaroo. It's found in Lesson 66. What letter does Keith's name start with? What sound does that make? Draw a circle, square, and triangle. Look at them and listen How many sides does a triangle have? Three. How many sides does a square have? Four. How many sides does a circle have? None! You can cut out the mom and baby kangaroo. Have a parent cut a slit for the pouch to slip the baby into from the back.

This page is blank for the cutting activity on the other side.

Ll

Lee
the
Lion

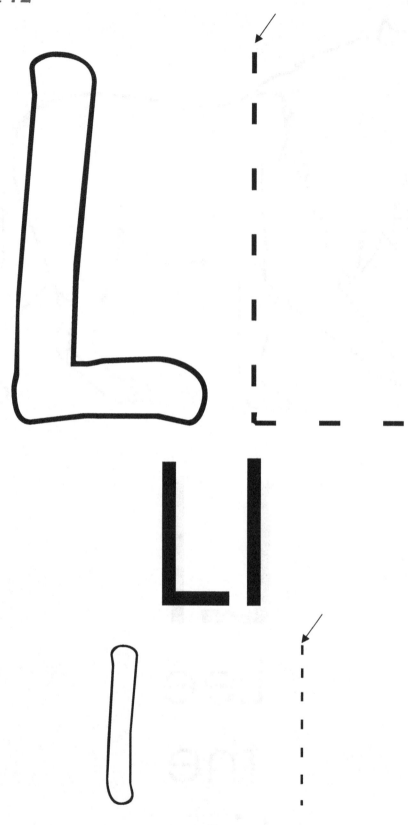

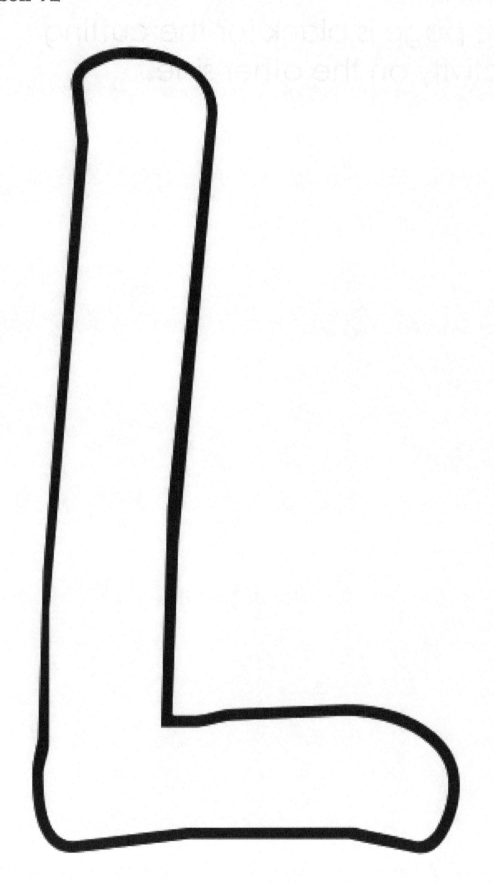

This page is blank for the cutting activity on the other side.

L l

Find the letters.

Llamas live in South America. They are used by people to carry loads. Llamas eat plants and don't need a lot of water.

Trace the curves. Start with the one in the top left. Start at the smiley face and trace around. Then move to smiley face next to it.

Love the LORD your God with all your heart and with all your soul and with all your strength.

This page is blank for the cutting activity on the next page.

You can cut out this lamb and glue on cotton balls.

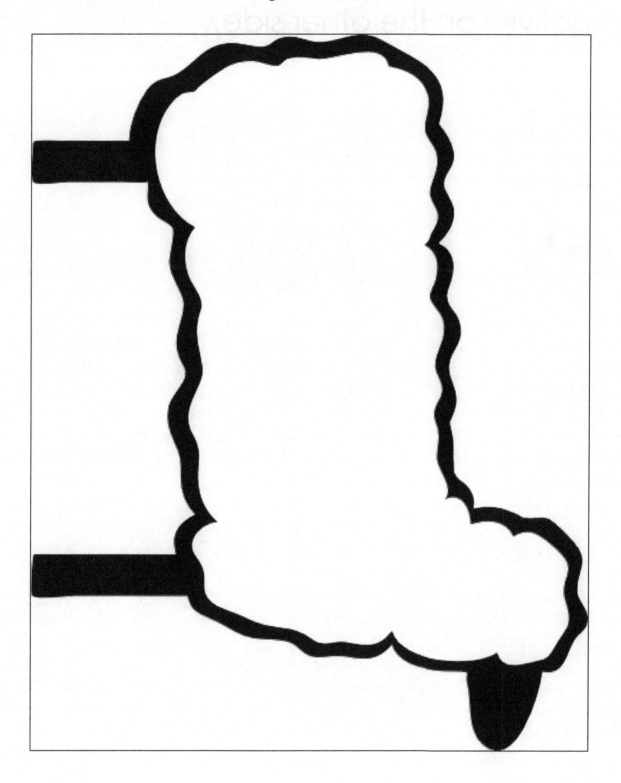

This page is blank for the cutting activity on the other side.

K k

Find the letters.

Koalas live in Australia. Koalas snack on eucalyptus leaves which are poisonous, but koalas have a trick to eating them.

This page is blank for the cutting activity on the next page.

Lesson 79

This page is blank for the cutting activity on the other side.

Lesson 80

Cut out the rectangles and lay them out or glue them together into the robot shape. I made the head a lighter color so you can give your robot a face!

This page is blank for the cutting activity on the other side.

Mm

Michelle the Monkey

M m
Find the letters.

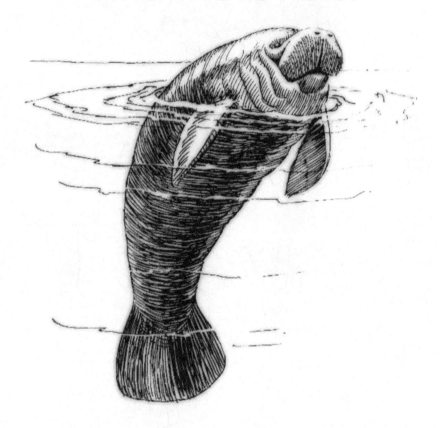

Manatees live in the ocean.
They are slow swimmers. They
move around in small groups.
Manatees are mammals.

"I am the Lord's servant," Mary answered. "May your word to me be fulfilled."

Trace each line. Start with the one in the top left corner. Start at the smiley face. Draw straight down and pick up your crayon or pencil when you get to the end of the dotted line and then jump up to the smiley face right next to it.

This page is blank for the cutting activity on the next page.

Put together this shape craft. Cut out each shape and glue them together onto a separate piece of paper.

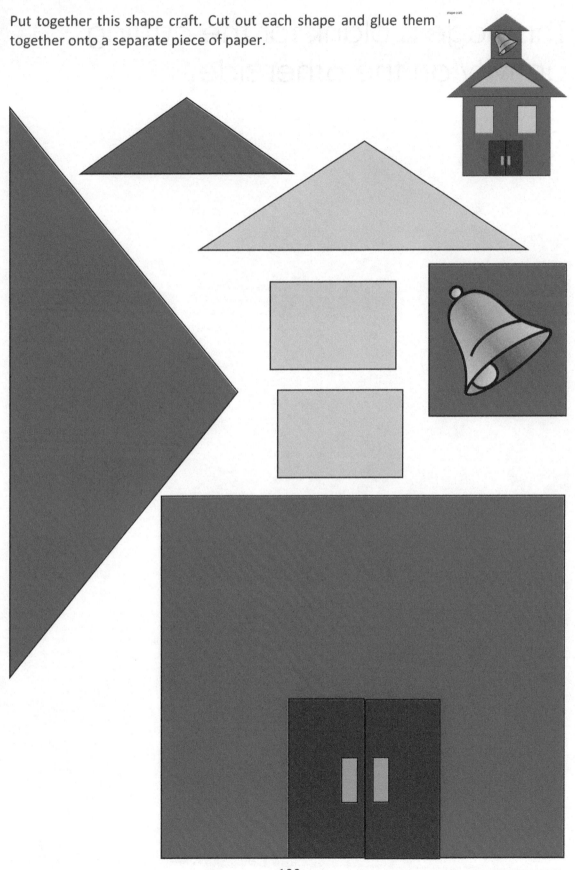

133

This page is blank for the cutting activity on the other side.

You can color this "M" in like a mountain. Leave the tips white, like a snow-topped mountain. Color the rest gray or green.

Nn

Nicole the Nuthatch

Never will I leave you nor abandon you.

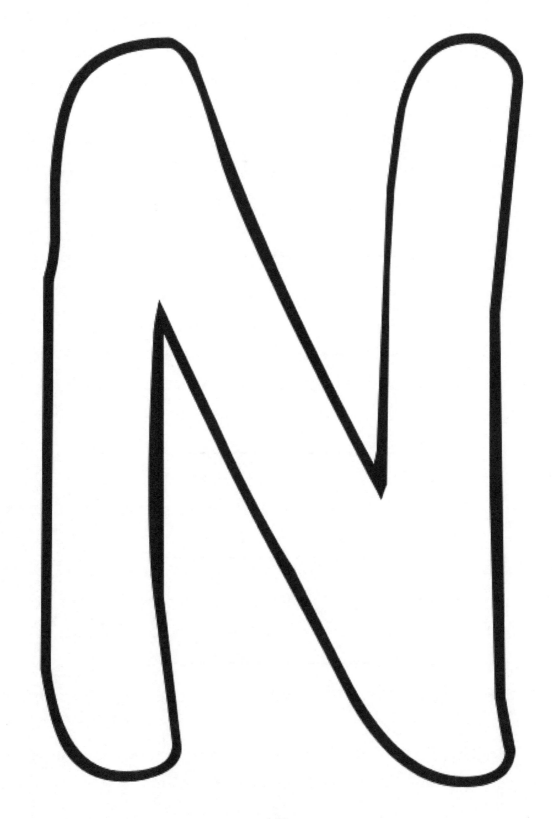

Go on a hunt for the Letter N. Can you find it around your house? What sound does it make? Listen again to the story of Nicole the Nuthatch. It is found in Lesson 86. Today you could make a nest. Take a paper bowl or a plastic bowl. If you want, you could paint it brown or glue on brown paper. You could also skip that part. Gather up nest materials and glue them onto your bowl. You could use grass, sticks, and leaves. You could also use yarn. Write an N on each egg and fill your nest.

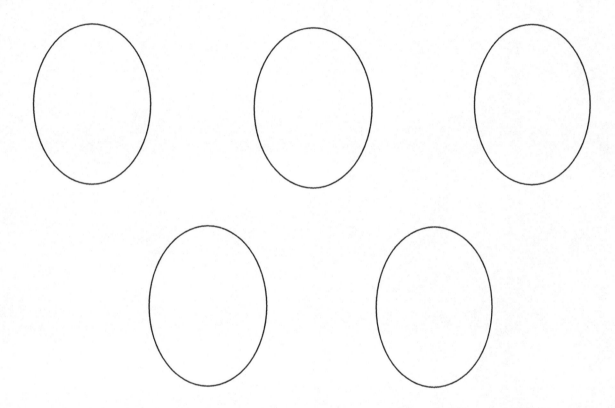

This page is blank for the cutting activity on the other side.

Oo

Olivia
the
Octopus

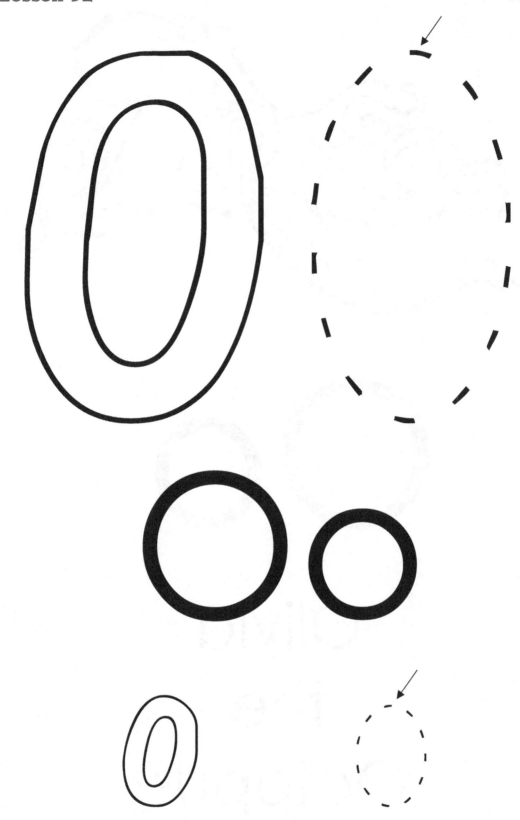

Find the letters.

Giant river otters can be six feet long. They live in the Amazon. Mostly they eat fish for their food. Otters are mammals.

Oh, give thanks to the Lord, for He is good!

Trace the circles starting at the smiley face in the top left and draw around the circle. Then move to the next circle. You can color the circles in with green and blue. The Letter O looks like a circle.

EP Preschool Printables
Lesson 94

Trace these lines. Start at the smiley face in the top left corner and draw down. Then jump up to the next one.

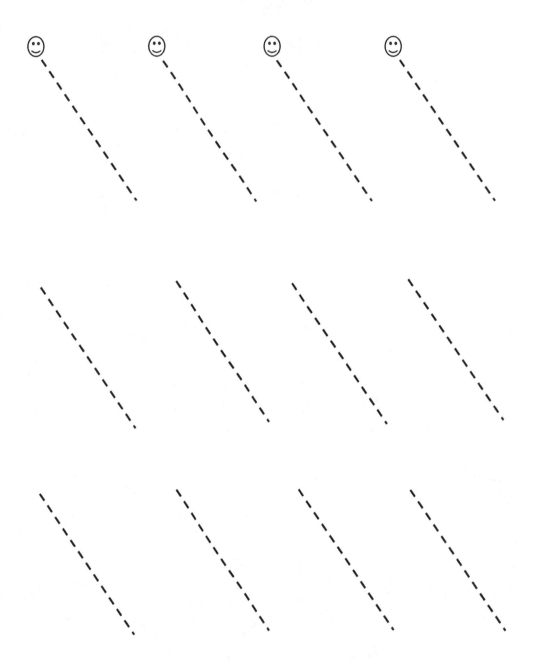

Draw on a face and eight legs. Or cut legs out of construction paper and glue them on if you like.

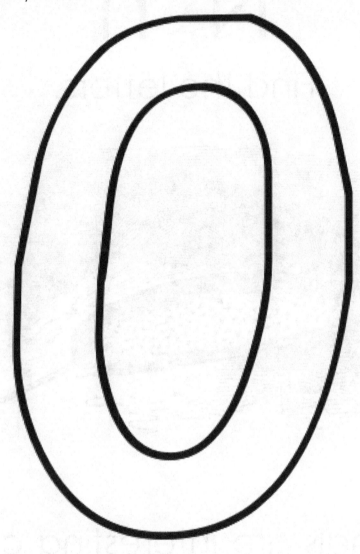

N n

Find the letters.

Narwhals are interesting ocean animals. They have two teeth. One grows into a tusk, a pointy sword coming from its mouth.

Cut out the shapes and make an ostrich. What sound does "ostrich" start with? "Ah" What letter makes that short vowel sound?

This page is blank for the cutting activity on the other side.

Pp

Paul
the
Parrot

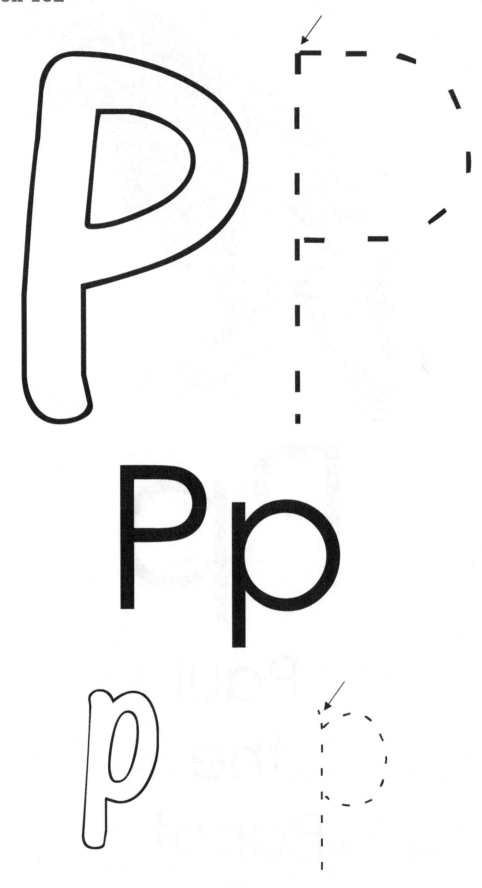

P p
Find the letters.

Giant pandas' place is in China.

People pick them out by their

color, but they are born white.

Pandas pick bamboo to eat.

Praise him with lute and harp! Praise him with strings and pipe!

EP Preschool Printables
Lesson 104

Trace the lines to practice your writing. Start with the smiley face in the top left corner. Draw down along the dotted line. Then pick up your pencil or crayon and move to the next one over. Always start at the top of the line.

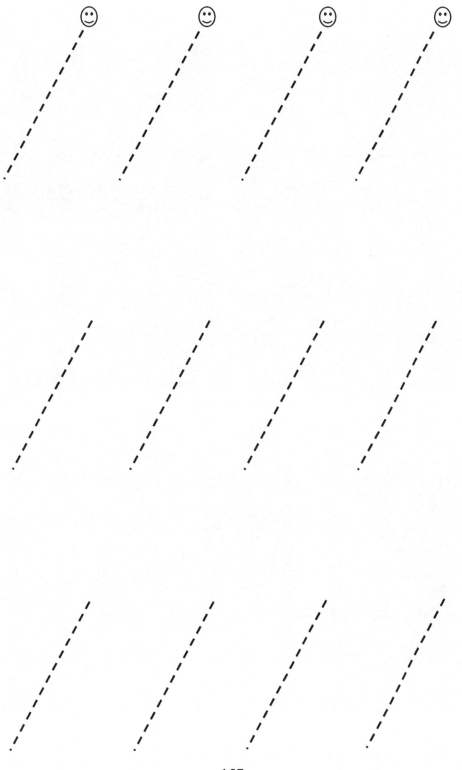

This page is blank for the cutting activity on the next page.

Today you can cut out these shapes and make a penguin. What sound starts penguin? What letters starts the word "penguin?" This penguin is made with ovals. You can draw on a face!

159

This page is blank for the cutting activity on the other side.

Qq
Queenie
the
Queen Bee

Trace around the circles with a pencil or crayon. Start with the one in the top left. Then move to the one next to it. Listen to the story of Queenie the Bee in Lesson 106.

Quit before the quarrel breaks out.

Quietly work with your hands.

This page is blank for the cutting activity on the next page.

You can put together a quilt. Here's a picture of a quilt. It's a blanket made out of squares or other shapes all put together. You can color in these shapes and cut them out and glue them onto another piece of paper to make your own unique quilt. You can also make your own shapes to use.

This page is blank for the cutting activity on the other side.

Rr

Robert
the
Rabbit

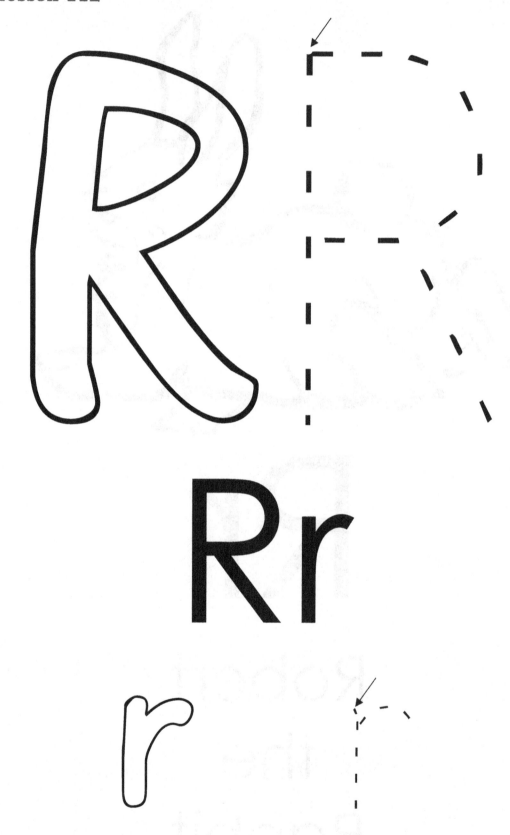

R r

Find the letters.

Racoons live all over, and they eat almost anything. After dark they use their front paws to grab the food they find.

Remember the wonders he has performed, his miracles, and the rulings he has given.

This page is blank for the cutting activity on the next page.

Cut out this square. Then cut a plain piece of paper in half longways. Attach the two strips together with tape or a stapler. Fit it to your head and then close the circle with tape or a stapler. Then attach the rabbit ears and wear then on your head. You can act out the story of Robert the Rabbit wearing your rabbit ears.

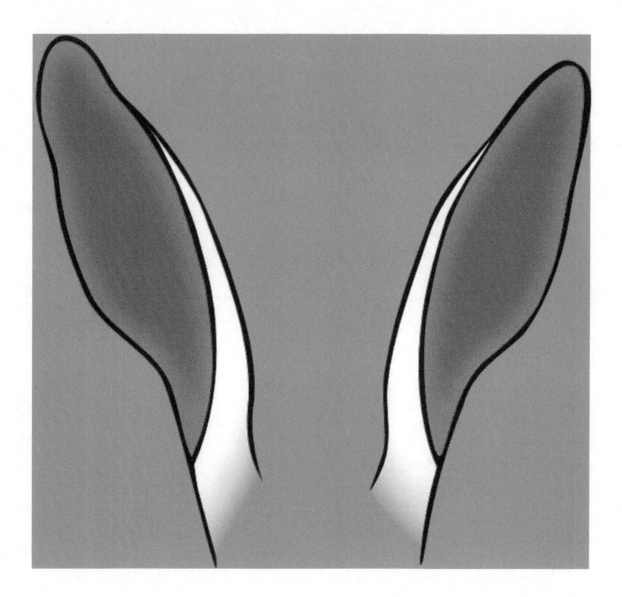

This page is blank for the cutting activity on the other side.

Color this rainbow. The colors in every rainbow go in a special order. It's labeled on the rainbow. It would be easiest, I think, to color up and down along each lane. You don't have to fill in every space, just show the colors in each part. Maybe you could color one side and whoever is working with you could color the other side and you could meet in the middle.

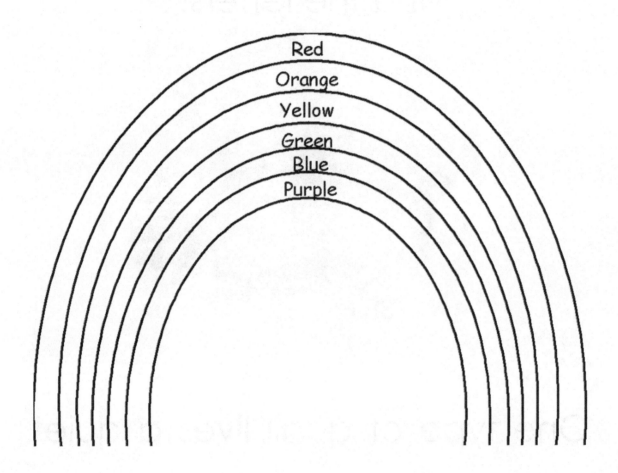

Q q

Find the letters.

One type of quail lives a quiet life in California. The male can be quite beautiful with a feather plume on his head.

Color the inside star in the shape below and then cut out the big star. It might be best to have a parent or older sibling cut around the inside star. You'll end up with two stars. Hold onto the smaller star for tomorrow.

This page is blank for the cutting activity on the other side.

Color the shapes. Cut out the shapes. Then you can tape yarn onto each point of the star. One piece will be to hang the star. The others can all hang down the other way and can each have a shape attached. Then glue your star from Lesson 119 onto the back of this star.

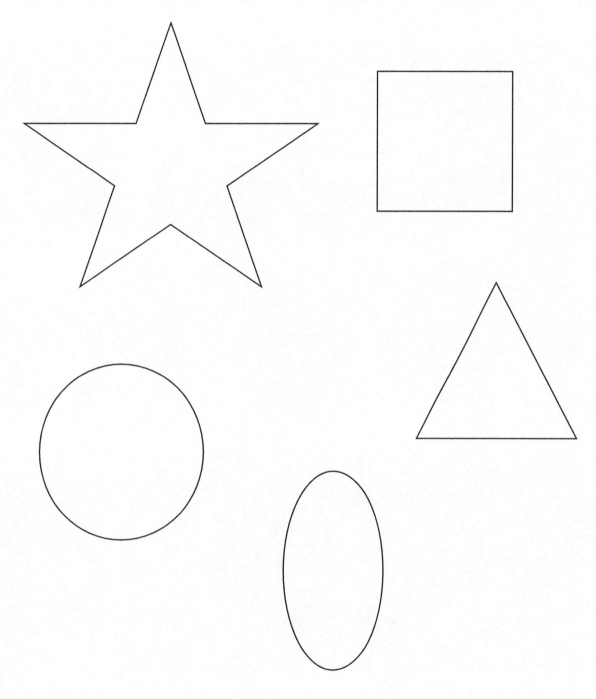

This page is blank for the cutting activity on the other side.

Ss

Sammy
the
Snake

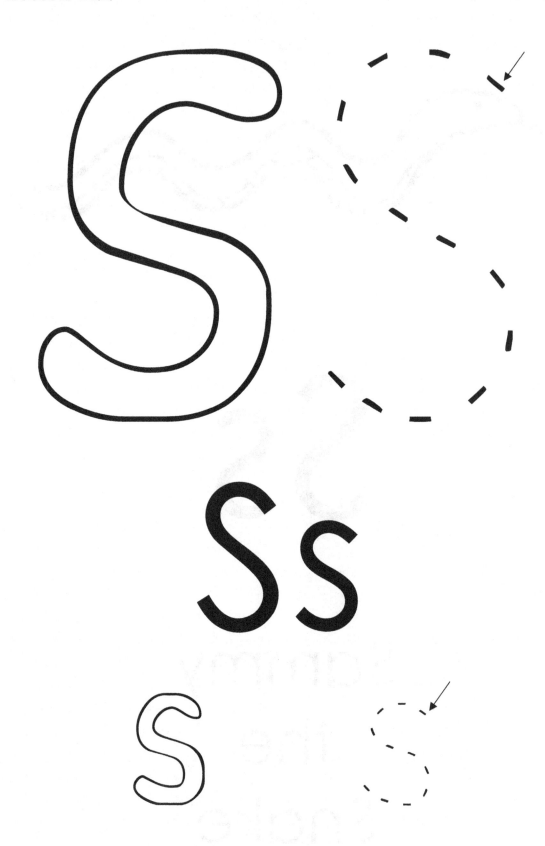

S s
Find the letters.

Skunks live in North America.
They are known for their smell
which they shoot in defense.
The scent is strong and awful.

Set your minds on things above, not on earthly things.

This page is blank for the cutting activity on the next page.

Cut out this rectangle. Fold it into thirds with the cover on front. In each section on the inside, draw one of the S-sound shapes: circle, star, square.

This page is blank for the cutting activity on the other side.

Tt

Timothy
the
Turtle

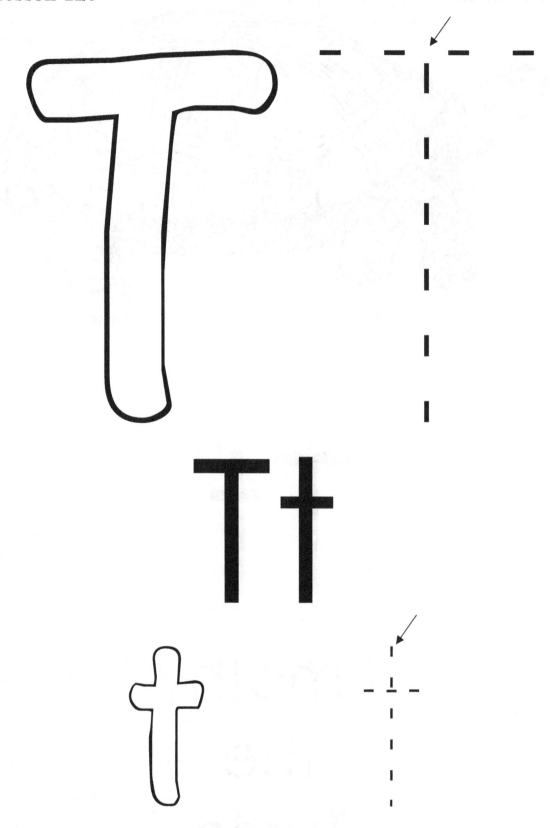

Trust in the Lord with all your heart.

Draw lines on this Letter T to make it look like train tracks. What sound starts the words train and track? What letter makes that sound?

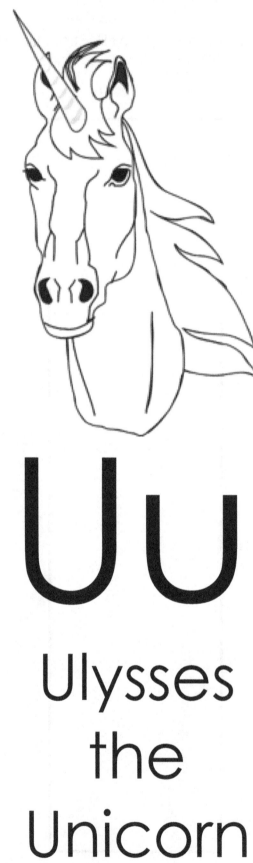

Uu
Ulysses
the
Unicorn

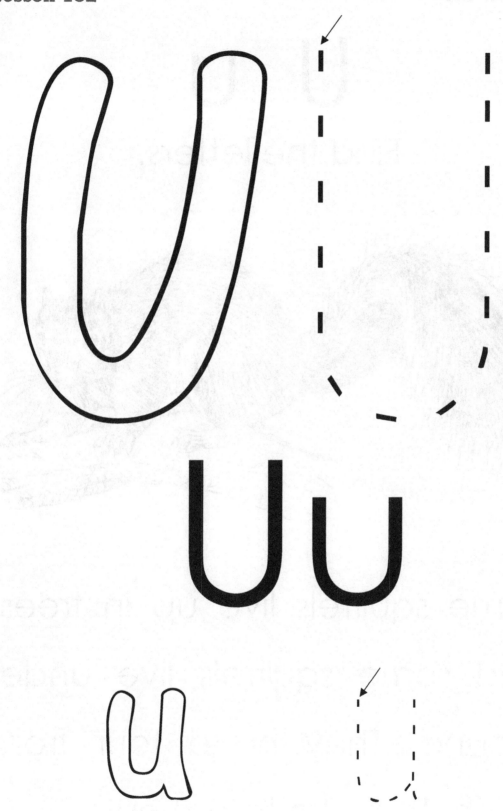

U u

Find the letters.

Some squirrels live up in trees, and some squirrels live under ground. They have four front teeth. They like to eat nuts.

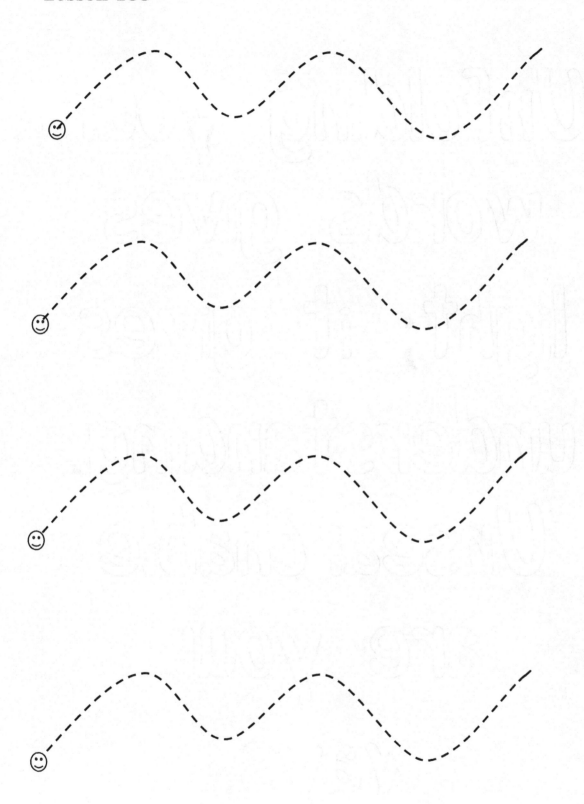

Unfolding your words gives light; it gives understanding. Unsearchable are your ways.

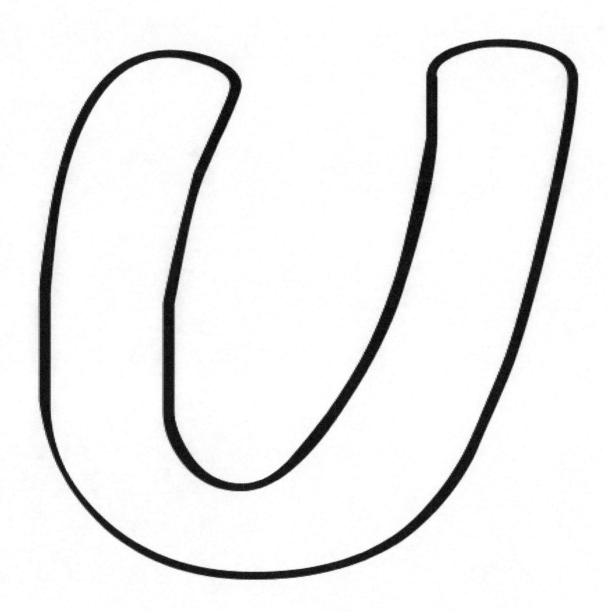

This page is blank for the cutting activity on the other side.

T t

Find the letters.

Tigers live in Asia. They are the largest kind of cat. They are targets for hunters. Tigers have a lot of strength.

Here is a snowman. Can you draw a square on his head and turn it into a hat? Can you draw circles on his face for eyes? Can you draw a triangle on his face for his nose? Then you can draw on arms, buttons, scarf, or whatever you like.

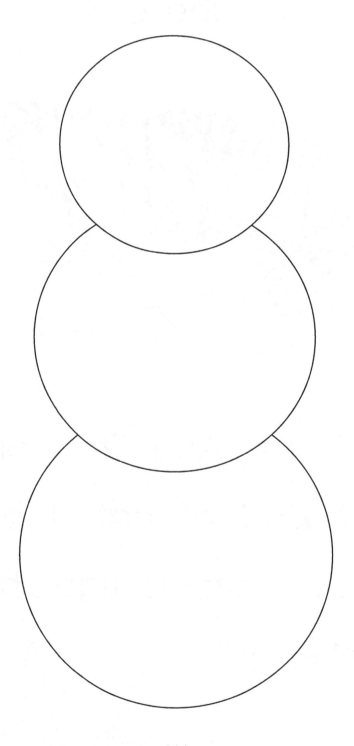

Vv

Victor
the
Vulture

V v

Find the letters.

Wolves live in the Northern Hemisphere, but there are areas in which they have not survived because they are killed.

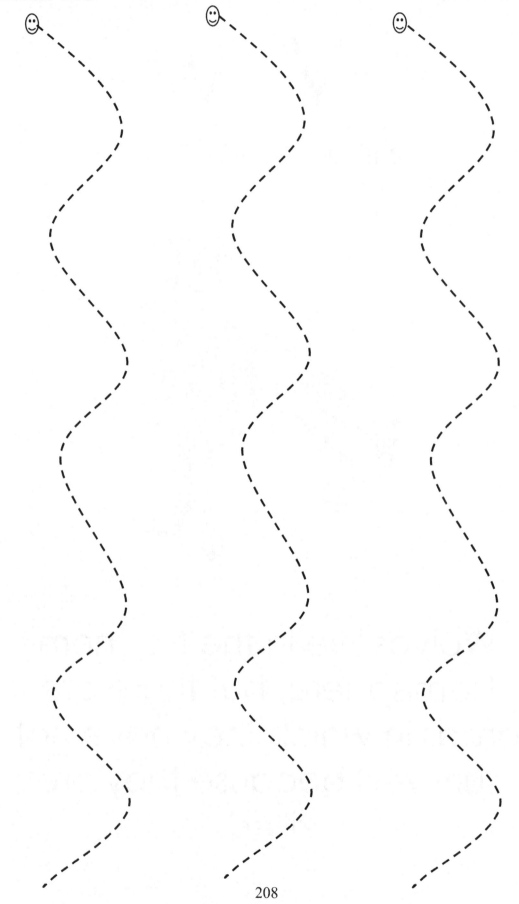

208

Victory in Jesus! The Word of God is alive and active, even dividing soul and spirit.

Turn this Letter V into a vase or a volcano. To make it a vase, color blue between the lines on the inside and then draw stems and flowers coming out of the water. To make a volcano, color brown down outside of the Letter V on both sides. Then make orange and red lava in the middle and spurting out the top.

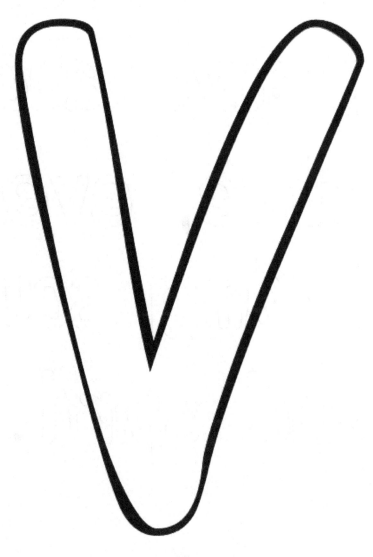

Ww

William
the
Walrus

When I am afraid, I will trust in You.

You will always be with me.

214

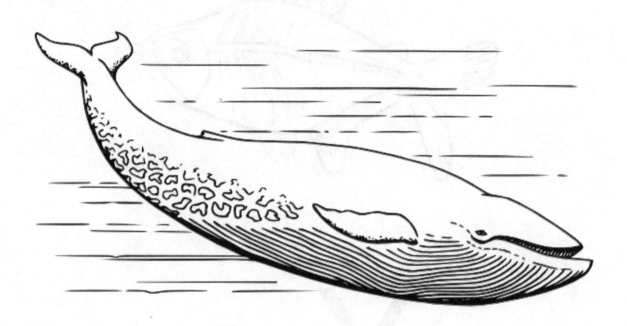

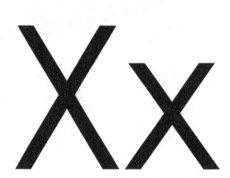

Xx

Xavier
the
X-ray Fish

I will exalt you, O God! Excellent is your name! You existed before all worlds.

X x

Find the letters.

The lynx live in northern forests.
They have extra thick fur coats
to keep them warm. Some lynx
are in danger of going extinct.

😊- - - - - - - - - - - - - - - - -

😊- - - - - - - - - - - - - - - - -

😊- - - - - - - - - - - - - - - - -

😊- - - - - - - - - - - - - - - - -

- - - - - - - - - - - - - - - - -

- - - - - - - - - - - - - - - - -

- - - - - - - - - - - - - - - - -

- - - - - - - - - - - - - - - - -

W w

Find the letters.

Blue whales live underwater.

They weigh as much as 100 cars.

In one day they can swallow

about two cars' worth of krill.

Their underside is white.

Yy

Yolanda
the
Yak

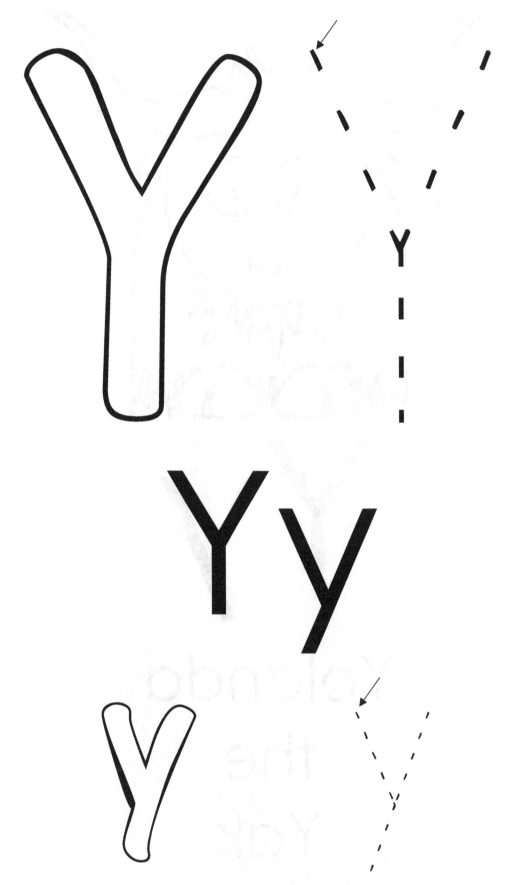

Y y
Find the letters.

The platypus is an interesting animal. They swim gracefully, but walk awkwardly on land. They lay eggs on land.

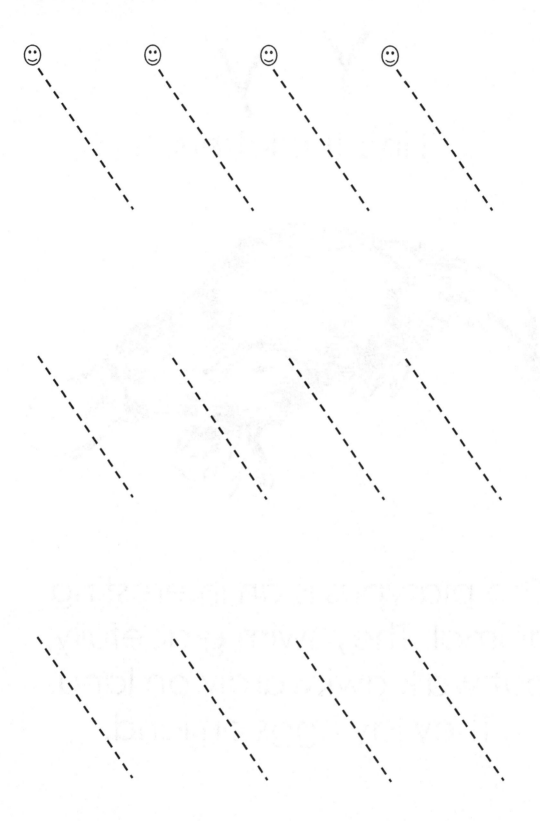

You, Jesus, are the same yesterday, today, and forever.

This page is blank for the cutting activity on the next page.

Sing the alphabet song. Listen again to Yolanda's story found in Lesson 161.
Cut out these shapes and make a yak! What shapes are on this page?

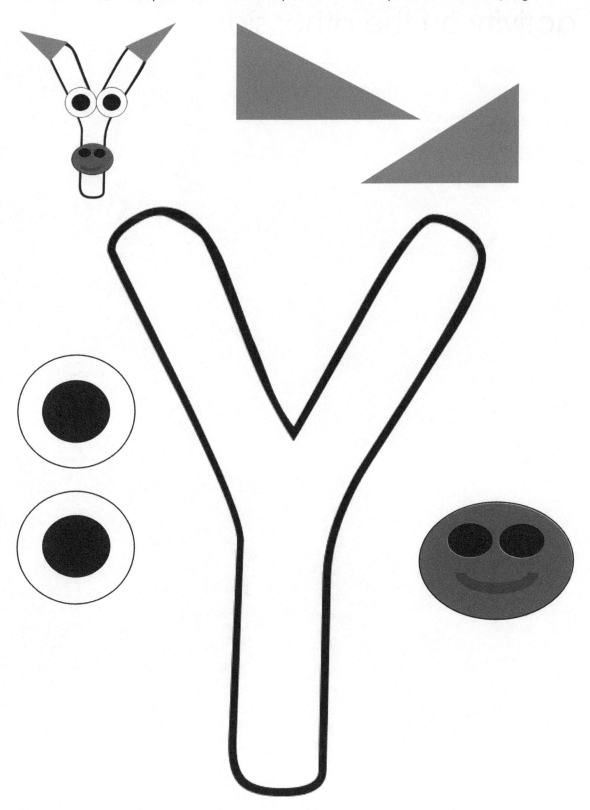

This page is blank for the cutting activity on the other side.

Zz

Zoe
the
Zebra

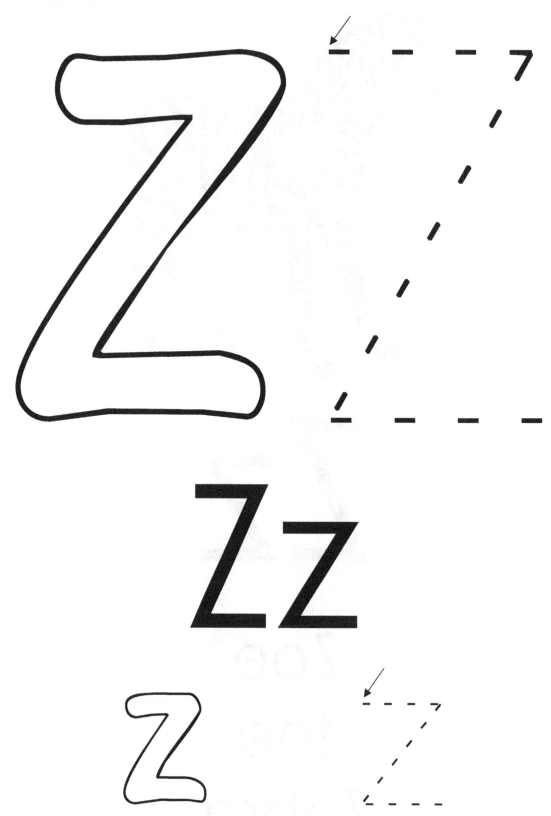

Z z

Find the letters.

Zebras live in Africa. They graze on grass. Each zebra has its own pattern of crazy stripes that confuse its enemies.

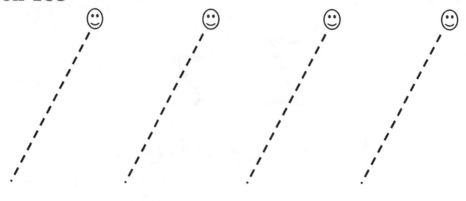

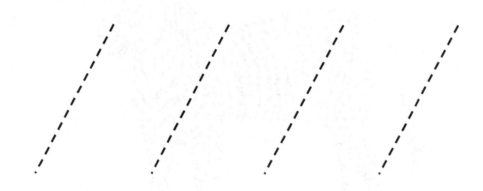

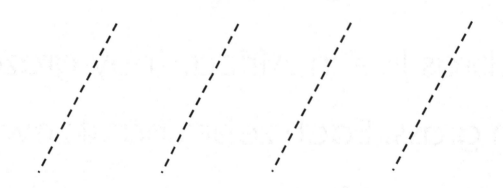

Zeal for My house in Zion burns in Me.

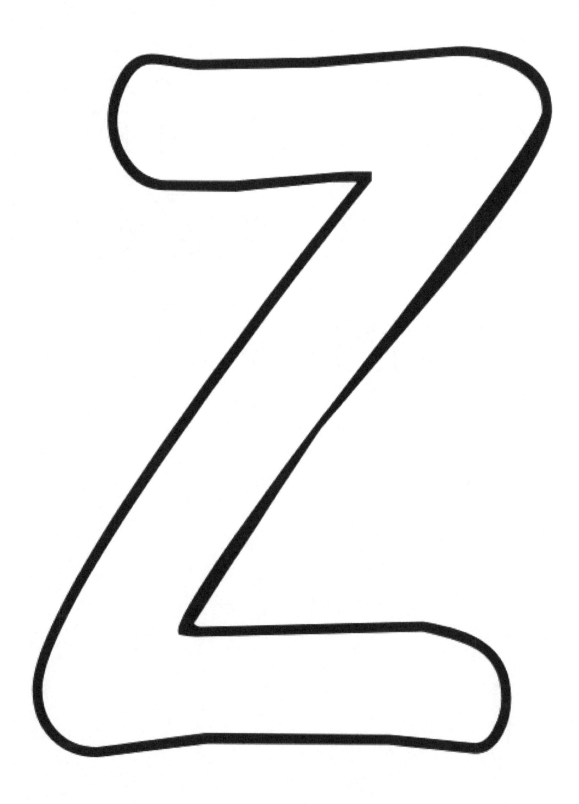

EP Preschool Printables
Lesson 171

Roll a die; when you land on a letter, say its name, sound, and a word that
begins with that letter. Make a mark or a post-it note to keep your spot.

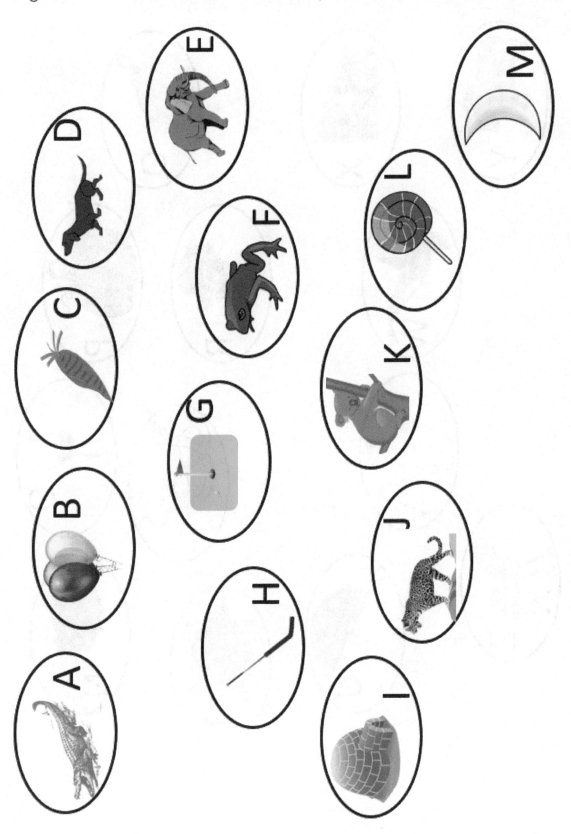

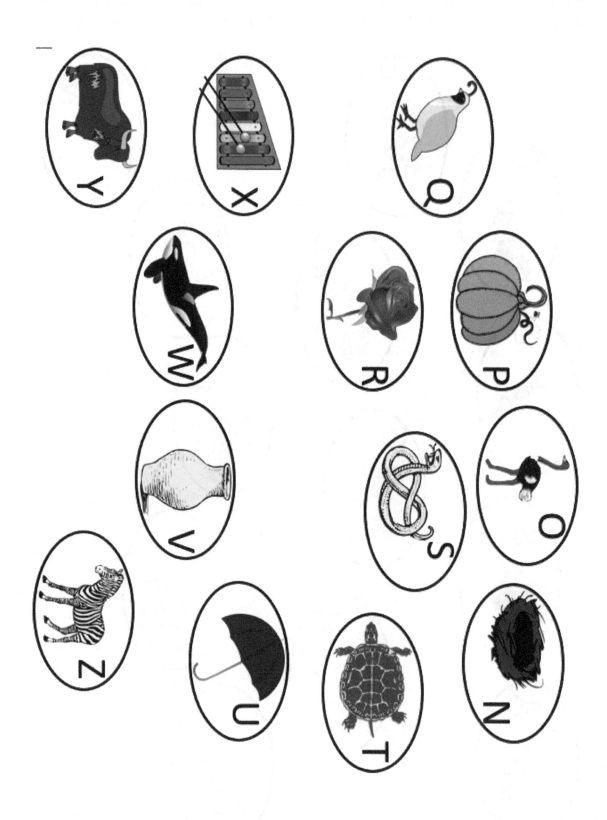

I hope you are enjoying learning with Easy Peasy All-in-One Homeschool. Once your child knows the alphabet letters and sounds, it's time to move onto the McGuffey Primer. If you'd like to work offline, consider getting our Learn to Read book which contains the sight words and reading lessons from the Primer.

Made in the USA
Las Vegas, NV
06 September 2023

77142226R00131